AF348528

TABLE OF CONTENTS ————————————

"We can all know everything without ever knowing how," is a quote from the song, "It's In Every One of Us," sung in the Science of Mind Church I attended for many years. Now, I really do believe we can all know everything; I also believe I understand how.

Soul Food for the 21ˢᵗ Century serves as a reminder for some, an introduction for others and a guide for all explaining the powers that are active and alive in every human Soul. It is easy to believe you have no power over your life's situations. It is even easier to blame someone or something for your current experiences. This book challenges the reader to test and prove their power to themselves.

Could you believe that **you, the human being, are more powerful than any technological advance or creation there is? Have you ever thought of yourself as powerful?** The Book of Genesis 1:26 states: then God said, "Let us make man in our image. And let them *have dominion over* the fish of the sea and over the birds of the air ... the domestic animals all over the earth, and all the animals that crawl on the earth." This gives *every human Soul* enormous power in ways that are not easily recognized or understood.

Human powers include the power of belief, the power of thought, the power of words, and more! To many, these will not seem like "powers," even though no animal, fish, fowl nor plant have these abilities. Human powers are always working at maximum potential. For instance, the power of belief is at work accepting, rejecting or judging the actions, ideas and commitments of the self and others all the time. Sometimes the power of belief gets confused with *control* when it comes to what others believe. The powers of thought and words are often used simultaneously in accordance with our motive and intention. In *Soul Food for the 21st Century*, I use personal experiences to share how I have misunderstood, misused, abused and have now been empowered by these Powers within me.

Power is defined as force, strength, might, the ability to perform effectively and having great influence. The same kind of powerful energy surrounds and permeates our words, our thoughts, our beliefs and all our powers and abilities within, continuously.

Not only do we have power, we have Free Will, which enables us to express ourselves however we wish. We are all born with knowledge of our **one** governing Law - known as the Law of Attraction or Law of Cause and Effect, karma or "what goes around, comes around." Law is designed to balance everything and every activity that takes place upon the planet. For every human, this means that there is a correspondence, a consequence or balancing that must happen for everything we do. *With total impersonality*, this Law makes each of us responsible for most of our life's experiences, whether we realize it or not!

Through poetry and prose, *Soul Food for the 21st Century* offers many ways to efficiently and effectively use your Soul powers to live the abundantly fulfilled life that was promised.

INTRODUCTION ——————————

Are you sure you're getting your minimum daily dosage of light, love, breath and life required to grow and maintain a vibrant, energized, well-nourished Soul? Did you know that the Soul, also known as Spirit or Spiritual body, lies deep within our physical existence? This is where it empowers and grows with, and as us. Were you aware that your Soul must be exercised, recognized and communicated with daily to continue being the animating force that fulfills your physical demands? Would you believe that it is the Soul who makes sure we receive all that we say, think, imagine, believe, demand and repeat?

If we are truly Spiritual beings living in a physical universe, as it is believed, then we should expect a life filled with physical experiences. However, the truth is, we are really spiritual beings, living in a spiritual universe, having spiritual experiences all the time, whether we believe it or not! You *can prove this* truth to yourself.

The purpose of *Soul Food for the 21st Century* is to assist in the process of building a more prosperous, productive, meaningful physical existence and to help us remember how to use our natural God-given powers and abilities with intention, to magnify and empower the Soul.

Soul Food for the 21st Century provides information on how to live from the spiritual perspective in this world, where everything appears totally physical.

Soul Food for the 21st Century is for those who have the desire to know just how powerful, how creative we are and can be; for those who believe that there's more to life than our current everyday experiences and for those who have the will to live more.

THE SOUL

According to the American Heritage Dictionary Second College Edition, the Soul is the animating and vital principle in man. The Soul is credited with the faculties of thought, action, emotion, and is considered the spiritual nature of man. The Soul is regarded as immortal, considered as perfect, in that it cannot be injured, diseased, damaged or destroyed. Soul expresses itself through one's character, personality, mind and separates from the physical body at death.

Matthew 10:28 –And fear not them which kill the body, but are not able to kill the Soul.

Soul is a Greek word derived from a verb "to cool, to blow" and hence refers to the vital breath, the animating principle in humans, animals, plants and other living, moving things. Soul and spirit may have different meanings for some, but are synonymous in this book.

Some schools of thought say the Soul is the conscience and that the conscience is energy, which has no form or location. Others think Soul is located in the heart or the aura, held there by electrical forces.

The Baghavad Gita tells us that the Soul is "one hundredth of one hundredth of the width of a human hair." Vedic wisdom points to electricity, more specifically, the electron, which cannot be captured. While the position of the Soul has not been located, it is believed that it moves freely and instantaneously throughout the body's electrical field.

While no one really knows where the Soul is located in the body, some writings, Vedic and otherwise locate the Soul at the base of the brain.

The pineal gland called "the seat of the Soul" by Descartes, sits in the geometric center of the brain. It lies directly behind the eyes, hence the biblical saying "the eyes are the windows to the Soul."

Keeping things simple, **Soul is the breath, the life force that GOD breathed into each of us. Spirit is the energy or breath of GOD that gives life to the Soul hidden within us all.**

If you have ever had an out-of-body or a near-death experience, you would understand that spirit really does move freely and instantaneously throughout the body's energy field, which apparently is quite large.

Soul Experiences

I lost control of my bicycle while traveling down a hill entering a parking structure. In just seconds, my speed went from 10 to 35 mph and I hit a concrete wall. Instantly I was out of my body, hovering in the ceiling above watching me all twisted up in my bicycle, and sliding slowly down the wall. I felt no pain, heard nothing, had no connection to my arms or legs, and felt like I was just a head or brain watching myself. I could see my cousin standing over my body. As she began to call me, I saw myself becoming alert, but still could not move. It was not until the firefighters began to untangle me that I was forced back into my body quickly, feeling excruciating pain from the experience. That time I was out of my body and still conscious.

Another time, I was hospitalized for uncontrollable blood sugar and a virus. I didn't know I had died. The nurse said, "She's turning blue." In that same second, I was looking down at my body from the ceiling. I felt nothing and could see my lifeless body on a bed that the nurse made do amazing things. She turned the hospital bed 180 degrees straight up from the bottom so my feet were in the air. People were busy working on my body. Although I felt nothing, I could hear a loud noise sounding like machinery.

The next thing I remember was the nurse telling me what a scare I gave them. While I was amazed at how she turned the bed around and upside down, I did not tell her. I did not share with her because of my own insecurity at the time.

During the time I learned to meditate, I briefly studied a principle called "Eckankar," which means co-worker with God. My interests led me to study a technique called Soul travel. The actual meaning of Soul travel is *moving into the higher realms of God,* but for me, it was more like meditation with purpose. Following the same guidelines as meditation, I was to call a master teacher by name and visit his spiritual training class that is always in progress. During my lunch hour, I would practice while sitting in my car.

One day I went so deep into meditation I became unconscious of the car and had no memory of where I went. Slowly becoming conscious again, I could hear someone calling my name. All of a sudden, I could see the person walking toward me in the distance and at the same time, I could see the top of my car. I then realized I was floating down to get into my body but she got to my car before I could get safely back. When she started banging on my car window to awaken me, it startled me and instantly I was back into my body. I was sure the severe headache I endured came from her interference.

We've all had experiences with our Soul and or spirit that we haven't understood, shared or given much attention. Maybe it's time we did.

PART ONE ——————————

Who we are as Spiritual Beings
The powers and benefits of Spiritual Beings
The laws that govern Spiritual Beings
Understanding Law
Using Law to benefit oneself

GOD-GIVEN POWERS

Every human being has received an exact set of the same Soul abilities and qualities also known as our God-given powers. How we use our God-given powers makes us appear different in many ways. Even though we have used them since birth, they don't seem like powerful abilities. However, what you believe, how you think and the words you choose to express yourself are three of your God-given powers. The powers of belief, thought and words are always working for or against you.

We all have natural imagination and intuitive ability albeit we may not choose to use or believe their powerful effects upon our life. The power of belief affects everything that happens in our lives. While it is not necessarily the first power one cultivates, nurtures and develops, the power of belief is one of the first powers one discovers.

Our God-Given Powers include:

Thought	A process of mind that is creative. Thoughts are energy. Thoughts turn into things. Thoughts begin like tiny bubbles and grow with each act of concentration, meditation and

imagination. Thoughts burst into reality with ample repetition.

Words
Words are energy, breath, sounds that symbolize meanings, communicate an assurance, a promise, a sworn intention, a command, an order or a direction. Words uplift, empower, nurture, heal, hurt, inspire, destroy, incite anger, joy and more.

Belief
Mental acceptance of a set of opinions, a doctrine, a habit of trusting, faith, confidence in a proposition. Beliefs provide the foundation for our lives.

Forgiveness
A physical act of giving up energy that returns light and energy fragments to the spiritual and physical body.

Meditation
A receiving and giving of energy to the spirit and Soul within.

Imagination
Restores and revitalizes our creative energy, empowers creative ability.

Intuition
An inner-natural knowing that intensifies with the practice of deep breathing, meditation, trusting the self and the thoughts and ideas that come to your mind.

Repetition
The power and energy behind every manifestation and demonstration. When we desire something, we think about it often, which is repetition of thought. Next, we speak about it again and again to whoever will listen, another aspect of repetition. The final act of repetition makes that desire the

reason for almost everything we do until we manifest.

Silence   Restores energy and creates substance.

In the Book of John 14:12, Jesus says, *"Verily, verily I say unto you, he that believeth in me, the works that I do shall he do also; and greater works than these shall he do, because I go unto my Father."* Jesus knew that if anyone could master their God-given powers as he had, then greater works would naturally be done.

Historically, we've all been told that we are sinners because of our continued disloyalty to God or disbelief in God. A sin is a transgression of Divine Law, a condition of estrangement from God, as in believing one is separate from God or that God's Law is separate and different from man's law.

The whole idea of sin is forgiven by announcing regularly, as Jesus did, "I can, of myself do nothing. It is God in me, doing all things through me here and now." Putting God at the heart of all our activities not only dismisses and forgives any idea of sin, it makes an announcement of absolute truth about who and what we are.

DIVINE ORDER

EVERYTHING IS ALWAYS IN DIVINE ORDER.
YOU DON'T EVEN HAVE TO BELIEVE THAT IT'S TRUE.
JUST REPEAT IT IN THE MIDST OF YOUR ACTIVITIES
AND IT WILL MAKE A BELIEVER OUT OF YOU.

DIVINE ORDER, DIVINE ORDER
REPEAT IT IS ALL WE CAN DO
EVERYTHING IS ALWAYS IN DIVINE ORDER
MAKING A BELIEVER AND A RECEIVER OUT OF YOU.

Power of Belief, Thought and Imagination

Divine Order represents the belief that God created this universe where we live, breathe and move. This makes everything divine or God-like in expression. Put another way, everyone and everything has the spark of God within, aware or not. Divine energy is throughout the entire planetary system. There is no place where God is not. Divine Order means there are no accidents, no mistakes and no coincidences ever in life. Everything that happens is supposed to happen.

To call, claim or acknowledge Divine Order is to admit that everything is already in its divine state, no matter how it appears to you or the world.

Whenever I prejudge things before thinking about it or as we say, "call it like I see it," that first judgment puts automatic delays on and stalls the process of Divine Order. So, when you say *Divine Order*, patiently wait and allow the absolute truth of all you must know regarding a situation to be revealed. Just when you least expect it, the energy of the situation changes and works itself out without you saying or doing another thing.

The norm was to call on everything except the divine and to make judgments on it all. However, when I practice remembering, "I am a Divine Being," Divine Order becomes a natural consequence allowing me to remain peaceful no matter what.

Because of the many ways one can be distracted or led into temptation, we must keep our consciousness in the here and now while affirming Divine Order.

The only way to know Divine Order really exists is to test the idea for yourself. Calling everything, everyone and every situation in your life Divine will inspire unexpected positive outcomes.

The Power of Belief

Belief is a mental act, a habit of placing trust in a person or a thing. Belief is mental acceptance of or conviction in the truth or actuality of something. To hold dear which means to love, to cherish, highly esteemed or regarded.

To believe is to accept as true or real, to expect, to think, to have confidence, trust and faith in the value or existence of a thing, to judge and to hold dear. To hold our beliefs dear means that some of our beliefs are important to us like precious jewels, even though they may not be serving us at the time. They are like family, they've always been there and no one is willing to change.

Our power of belief is explained in the Bible. Mark 11:23-24 reads; "For verily I say unto you, that whosoever shall say unto this mountain, be thou removed, and be thou cast into the sea, and shall not doubt in his heart, but shall believe that those things which he saith shall come to pass; he shall have whatsoever he saith. Therefore, I say unto you, what things, soever ye desire, when ye pray believing that ye shall receive them, ye shall have them."

Where Beliefs Come From

Beliefs are inherited from parents, from our race, our culture, geographical location, friends, peers, teachers, books, the Internet, songs, the media and more. We have beliefs we are unaware of until confronted, otherwise they could remain dormant in our unconsciousness.

How Beliefs Continue

We are constantly bombarded from advertising media, commercials, news media, posters, signs, songs, billboards, newspapers, TV, Internet, radio, movies, subliminal music at malls and grocery stores. How many times can you watch or hear the same commercial without singing the jingle or repeating the script? This is how new beliefs are accepted and before you realize it, that product you were singing about is on your shelf. Once again, all beliefs become the building blocks of our reality.

What We Believe

We all have beliefs about absolutely everything. Our beliefs become opinions and judgments that we hold onto about illness, death, sex and age. Most of us have basic beliefs like life is hard and we say, "It's always something or if it ain't one thing, it's another." We believe we catch colds, flu and disease and when we do we say, "When it rains, it pours!" The one basic universal belief that earns billions of dollars is, "I live in an unsafe universe or my world or environment is not a safe place." The belief that slows down and sometimes stops achievements altogether is, "I am not worthy." This bottom-line belief hides in our excuses, our actions, our reasoning ability and has affected all of us at some time.

Changing a Belief

Belief is among our mightiest of God-given powers. The power of belief is our direct link to Law. Not only are beliefs made up of opinions and judgments, they serve as our choice and decision on a matter. We choose to believe certain things and consequently we receive what we believe in our experiences. Choosing to change a belief requires meditation, an understanding of Law, some specifically designed affirmations and your power of repetition combined with will power. Some beliefs are more embedded in our minds than we know and will require time, patience and effort to change.

THE LAW

DOES ANYONE RECALL THAT SPIRITUAL LAW?
THE ONE THAT MEANS YOU REAP WHAT YOU SOW?

IT ALSO MEANS "CAUSE AND EFFECT" AND FOR SOME,
WHAT GOES AROUND, COMES AROUND, YOU KNOW.

EVER WONDER? WHY DID THIS HAPPEN TO ME?
OR—WHAT DID I DO TO GET THIS?
WELL—THERE'S A CONSEQUENCE FOR EVERY THOUGHT,
WORD AND DEED
AND FOR THE THOUGHTS WE THOUGHT WE HAD DISMISSED.

CAUSE IS WHAT YOU DID, WHAT YOU THOUGHT, WHAT YOU
SAID.
EFFECT IS WHAT IS COMING BACK AT YOU.
IS IT GOOD? IS IT BAD?
IS IT HAPPY? IS IT SAD?
LOOK AT YOUR LIFE. SEE WHAT YOU'VE CREATED FOR YOU.

THERE'S GREAT POWER FOR ALL
WHO UNDERSTAND THIS LAW.
IT PUTS US IN CHARGE OF ALL THAT WE RECEIVE.
WHATEVER YOU THINK OR SAY, HOW YOU ACT AND TREAT
OTHERS
COMES BACK TO YOU. WHETHER OR NOT YOU BELIEVE.
THIS LAW KEEPS PERFECT ORDER IN EVERYTHING THAT
EXISTS.
RESPONSIBILITY IS ALWAYS THERE FOR YOU.
WAKE UP! BECOME AWARE OF WHAT YOU SAY AND WHAT YOU
THINK
AND EVERY LITTLE THING THAT YOU DO!

THERE'S GREAT POWER FOR ALL WHO UNDERSTAND THIS
LAW.
IT PUTS US IN CHARGE OF ALL THAT WE RECEIVE.
MAKE LIFE GOOD IF IT'S BAD,
MAKE IT HAPPY IF IT'S SAD,
IT'S GIVEN UNTO US AS WE BELIEVE.

There's great power for all who understand this Law
It puts us in charge of All that we receive
Make your life good if it's bad
Make your life joyous if it's sad
It's given unto you as you believe.
It's the Law!

Power of Words, Intuition and Belief (Law)

We must first understand that as Divine Beings we are naturally Spiritual Beings, part of and subject to Spiritual Law. To be spiritual means to possess the nature of Spirit or God. Spirit is that vital principle within us, that animating force or our breath. Our Spirit or Soul then, is our breath, our words and our God or air within. When we die, it is our spirit or our breath, that animating force within which leaves the body.

Since we are spiritual beings encased in a body that makes us human, we must obey Spiritual Law as well as the law of man. Spiritual Law never changes or adjusts in any way; however, the laws of man are unstable, can be changed and are amended frequently.

The Bible states in Isaiah 55:11, "*So shall my word be that goeth out of my mouth. It shall not return unto me void (unfulfilled), but it shall accomplish that which I please and it shall prosper in the thing whereto I send it.*" Simply put, this means that our words return to us in accordance with the same energy/motive used to think, and speak them.

Because we have a Soul or God within, we possess that same creative energy. Positive brings positive returns; negative returns negative and not to the person, place or thing we direct our energy to, but back to us the sender. Another way to express this is that a fragment of our Spirit goes out with and on every word we speak attracting its equivalent and returns it to us.

Far removed from traditional religious thought, I began to practice and study Universal Spiritual Law. I became enthralled with Universal Law, known then as *New Thought*. Reading about the Law agreed with and satisfied something within my Soul and the more I read, it became clear to me that the Law and God are one and work the same way.

The fact that God gives us free will to choose to obey Law or not makes perfect sense to me. It really does not matter what our race is, if we are old, young, rich, poor or if we obey Law or not; we are all forever governed by and subject to the Law of Cause and Effect.

We all discovered how Law works as an infant through sounds. It did not take us long to teach our parents what each of our sounds meant. We moved on to discover taste, touch, right and wrong early in life. By age 10, we all knew something about reaping and sowing from our experiences; however, it takes longer to realize that everything we do has a consequence.

At first, it seemed easier to recognize Law by observing how it was working in other peoples' lives. I cautioned my friends not to repeat negative things, like "I'm going to be sick tomorrow," "I'm getting old," "Arthr (short for arthritis) is setting in." I advised them to keep their words positive. I stopped reading newspapers, listening to and watching the news; in fact, I locked my TV away in a closet! Finally, I wouldn't allow my friends to relay bad news to me. If they had nothing positive to say, they simply could not visit or talk to me. Because I really meant it, many of them stayed away thinking I had become a fanatic! I believed that if I really had to know something, the universe would alert me in some way and it did!

A completely new world of learning had taken place for me and I was like a sponge, I spent all my free time reading spiritual books and practicing meditation. Through reading and practice, I was beginning to understand how *my* thoughts, *my* words, *my* actions, as well as *my* motives for doing what I did … *activates* the Law of Attraction!

Now remember, Law is *always* right there listening and acting upon every thought, word or deed. Have you ever questioned why things happen to *you* or what *you* may have done to cause a certain experience? The way to know that you are a *co-creator* is to consciously use or test Law. When we examine our own life, we can question recent events or things that have happened by asking Law to reveal itself in one situation at a time.

I recall being told as a child that only crazy people talked to themselves. However, I have caught me talking to myself many times, even though I know I'm not crazy or unstable. So yes, we must find a private place where we can speak out loud to ourselves, asking questions and demanding answers. Communicating with the self in this manner is helpful in clearing and calming the mind.

The best part is Law can be used to our advantage. We can change our thoughts and our words to become more uplifting and helpful and we can revise our motives to benefit ourselves and others.

When making a decision, one way to use Law is to ask yourself out loud, *what are the consequences if I say yes, or no?* Then listen to your heart, pay attention to everything and everyone around you, listening and looking for a sign or answer to your question. Expect an answer! Don't doubt the thoughts and ideas that come to your mind as your answer. Remember, you are never wrong, nor will your Soul ever give you wrong information.

Treating others in the same way we would like ourselves to be treated (respectful or not) and being conscious of what is happening in our lives (peace or drama) is another way to observe how we are using Law.

All of the above information can be considered the "tip of the iceberg" when becoming and remaining conscious of Law. It takes continuous practice to remember that our every thought, every word and everything we do is governed by Law.

Personal Mis-use of Law

I had just started dating a man who was divorced with shared custody of a disabled child. After a month or more of dating, he told me he'd like to help me make a little gas money. I listened as he explained that money was available through an agency that funded schooling, transportation, after-school activities and caregiver hours he was offering to me. All I had to do was fill out the weekly paperwork and mail it in, even though I would never meet or take care of his child. He made it sound like a gift since he could authorize and hire me. I was too busy thanking God for this "wonderful thoughtful man" to think about Law or consequences.

With this extra money coming bi-weekly, I invested in a used car. The car worked like a charm until I got my first paycheck for work I was not doing. The car was fine getting me wherever I had to be, but the engine would die before I could get back home. I had it towed to one repair shop three days in a row before just leaving it there. The mechanics never found a problem and my boyfriend was always around to comfort me during the breakdowns. I was too distracted to pray. Finally, after weeks of car problems that amounted to hundreds of dollars, I got some alone time to meditate, pray and ask why I was having to put out so much money! My answer came before I finished asking. In my heart I heard, "You are stealing; You are lying and accepting money for it." And because I know and claim to practice Law, I felt ashamed and foolish, but grateful for the realization.

There was nothing for me to say, I couldn't get upset with him because all I had to say was no. After a very sorrowful cry, thousands of "I forgive myself," and "I am alert, awake and aware of my actions," I quit the job and donated the car unknowingly to the same agency I had lied to and from whom I had stolen.

Instead of me quitting the boyfriend, I stuck around thinking I liked him, but looking back it was for another lesson in Law.

One thing I had learned from him was to listen carefully. When his cable was disconnected for non-payment, he ordered new service in his ex-wife's name, giving the cable company her social security number as well as important information belonging to her. This bothered me because he has been divorced more than 10 years. I knew this information meant there was no future in this relationship. I knew that consequences for knowing and continuing to date him would be even more detrimental for me. To his shock and dismay, I ended the relationship and moved on.

The phrase, "God or Law is no respecter of persons," simply means that Law or God must always balance no matter who or what. Law works the same for all without regard for race, status, religion, political affiliation or anything considered above man's law. There is always a consequential balancing everyone experiences for the things we do, say, think or intend.

Because of all the things we think, do and say unconsciously, it is close to impossible to figure why or what caused any of our experiences. Even with years of study and practice, it still took several months to begin to remember to stay alert, awake and conscious while talking or doing things.

PART TWO ———————

Thoughts, Ideas, Things Requiring Soulful Consideration ...

YOUR WORD

IT'S YOUR WORD THAT GIVES YOU MERIT.
IT'S YOUR WORD THAT SHAPES YOUR WORLD.
ALL YOU WILL EVER HAVE IS YOUR WORD.
SO, HOW WOULD YOU DESCRIBE YOUR WORD?

CAN YOU STAND ON IT WHEN ALL ELSE FAILS?
CAN YOU TAKE IT TO THE BANK?
CAN OTHERS?
CAN YOU REMEMBER YOUR WORD?
CAN YOU TRUST YOUR WORD?
WOULD YOU SAY
IT'S WORTH ITS WEIGHT IN GOLD?
CAN OTHERS SAY YOU ARE TRUE TO YOUR WORD?
CAN YOU?

HOW WOULD YOU DESCRIBE YOUR WORD?
BECAUSE, IT'S YOUR WORD THAT GIVES YOU MERIT.
IT'S YOUR WORD THAT SHAPES YOUR WORLD.
ALL YOU WILL EVER HAVE IS YOUR WORD.

The Power of Words

One way to deflate the power connected to your words is to lie either by intentional deceit or simply by telling someone you will do something with or for them and you don't follow through. My parents taught us that all you ever have is your word. That's how people did business with each other before written contracts. A person's word was their bond. You could depend on it. Many people who don't believe their words have power must also realize that we can only experience what we believe. How important are your words to you? When you make a promise to yourself, do you follow through? If your words represent you, how important are you to you?

In Matthew 12:37, Jesus said, *"for by thy words, thou shalt be justified, and by thy words, thou shalt be condemned."* This statement proves that **true power really lies in our words**!

Had I been raised to believe my every word had the power to save or condemn me, I would have been taught to carefully choose uplifting words to describe myself, my life and my desires. I would have received lessons at home on the importance of word origins and meanings. I would know not to use curse words, not to call myself or others dumb, stupid, jackasses, bitches or other offensive names. I would know to think before I speak, not lie, to listen and pay attention to myself and others when talking. I would remember to avoid getting caught up in conversations I'd regret. I would not talk against others or gossip. I would not use slang or "hip" talk. I would always think of myself as abundantly fulfilled.

Since I was not raised this way, I must now unlearn most of what I thought I knew, and everything I believed.

Many intelligent people believe their words can be given a meaning that they choose, one that is to their liking. This is simply **not true!** ALL words have an original or universal meaning also known as the "God-given" meaning, which cannot be changed, replaced or removed. It is important to know origins and meanings of the words you choose, to know the kind of energy you are calling to yourself through conversation and thought. **Yes, you have that kind of power!**

OUR POWER IS IN OUR WORDS

IT'S NOT SOME THINGS—IT'S EVERYTHING!
EVERY WORD WE SAY COMES BACK TO US.
CAUSE AND EFFECT - MAKES IT THAT WAY.
YOUR CHOICE OF WORDS IS YOUR CHOICE—
BUT IT MATTERS WHAT YOU SAY.

POSITIVE, NEGATIVE, RIGHT OR WRONG—
DIDN'T YOU KNOW? HAVEN'T YOU HEARD
WELL, IT'S IN YOUR MOUTH, IN THE WORDS THAT FLY OUT—
OUR POWER IS IN OUR WORDS.

WHEN WE BLESS, CURSE OR PRAISE
WHATEVER IS IN OUR VIEW,
WE CREATE A MAJOR CONSEQUENCE
AFFECTING OTHERS—BUT MOSTLY YOU.

IT'S NOW TIME TO BECOME AWARE
OF WHAT WE SAY AND WHAT WE THINK—
IF WE LISTEN TO OURSELVES—WE'LL REALIZE
IT'S OUR THOUGHTS THAT MAKE OUR LIVES STINK.

WHETHER IT'S POSITIVE, NEGATIVE, RIGHT OR WRONG—
LET'S NOT JUDGE—LET'S OBSERVE.
AND LET'S PAUSE BEFORE WE OPEN OUR MOUTHS
BECAUSE OUR POWER IS IN OUR WORDS.

Power of Words, Power of Thought

As Spiritual Beings, the words we speak have amazing drawing power and come back to us full of our motives combined with the God-given power naturally contained within each word. The Law of Attraction returns our words to us with the same intention that we sent out with them. It's just that we have had billions of thoughts and have spoken billions of words, it's hard to recall all that we have said and thought. Even though this same thing is happening to each of us all the time, many of us don't connect the situations in our lives to our words, thoughts or beliefs.

Beliefs, thoughts, imagination, words and more activate the Law of Cause and Effect; also known as the Law of Attraction, which goes to work **immediately** in our lives. Law is a consistent activity of Spiritual Beings. Understanding the power of words as one of our most vital powers is difficult. When we're really honest with ourselves, understanding the power of words means we can no longer blame others for the things we experience. Each one must **take responsibility** for calling "good and bad stuff" to our lives through our misuse or misunderstanding of Law and our own power.

Words Affect Us

There is enormous power in the words we choose and the effects they have on our emotions, our mentality, our physical body and our lives.

There was a very popular song recorded in the 1980's by a female artist with the hook of the song being, "I'm going crazy!" My friend's 17-year old son played the song repeatedly. He put so much energy in singing, "I'm going crazy," that I couldn't help but ask him to stop! When I explained how powerful his words were, he and his mother laughed at me, called me a crazy fanatic and "it's just a song," they said. I visited them a few months later only to find that her son had been committed to a mental institution for a nervous breakdown. Even though, the first thing that popped up in my mind was the word "crazy" and that song, I kept quiet. I knew that she would never make the connection between a song and his experience. This is true for most of us.

Test for yourself. Prove the power in **your words** and **your thoughts** by remembering some words you say often and by being attentive to the thoughts you tend to think over again and again. Then compare those words and thoughts to what you are experiencing in your life.

ATTITUDE

PEOPLE SAY I'M EVERYTHING
BECAUSE I AM ATTITUDE!
I'LL USE ALL OF YOUR BODY TO EXPRESS MYSELF
IN WHATEVER MANNER I CHOOSE.
I AM THE WAY YOU HOLD YOUR HEAD,
I AM SEEN IN YOUR EYES,
I'LL EXPRESS MYSELF THROUGH YOUR VOICE -
WHICH I CAN EASILY DISGUISE.
I CAN BE SEEN THROUGHOUT YOUR BODY,
I'M IN THE WAY YOU MOVE YOUR HANDS.
I BECOME EXTREMELY VISIBLE
WHEN I MAKE YOUR BODY STAND.
I KNOW IT SEEMS AS IF I AM EVERYTHING
AND I AM!
I AM REALLY THE PERCEPTIONS YOU PROJECT.
I AM YOUR AURA — SO DON'T FORGET.
ATTITUDE IS EVERYTHING!

Power of Thought, Power of Words

Attitude is energy. Attitude is seen in the body, on the face, heard in the voice and in the expression of feelings. Without realizing it, attitude is a state of mind. Ever heard the expression, "That's the attitude talking?"

We often fail to realize that our attitude reveals to others who we are, what we think and how we feel about everything that confronts us. Attitude is a condition as well as a state of belief. Many of us think we can hide our true feelings within, but our attitude is very hard to control or conceal.

We think we can cover our attitude by our actions or by the things we say, however, it shines even brighter as we lie. No matter what we think … attitude cannot be hidden! Our attitude is what makes a person feel comfortable or not around us. We are able to feel and see all the vibrations stemming from attitude!

Attitude is a garment. We are either aware that we are wearing it or not. To become aware of my attitude I gave attention to how I felt when I was happy, angry, sad, upset, positive, negative or not. All of this and more is expressed through body, eyes, face and actions whether we know it or not. It is so helpful to have a friend tell you when your attitude changes.

I have used my morning attitude to determine the flavor of my day. I always feel good in the mornings, but sometimes a disagreement from the day before may still be on my mind. If unable to turn it into a positive or keep my thoughts peaceful, I may avoid confrontation with that person or decide to stay home until I can change my energy.

Attitude is a powerful energy and has everything to do with our choices.

I Am

LISTEN MY CHILDREN
AND YOU SHALL HEAR
HOW NOW IS THE TIME
TO LIVE YOUR LIFE WITHOUT FEAR.

JUST REMEMBER THIS ONE SPIRITUAL LAW—
WHEN YOU SAY "I AM,"
IT'S GOD THAT YOU CALL.

WHAT YOU ADD TO "I AM"
BECOMES YOUR PRAYER.
POSITIVE, NEGATIVE,
LAW IS RIGHT THERE.

TEACH YOURSELF TO REMAIN AWARE
THAT GOD GIVES US WHATEVER WE DECLARE.

"I AM" MEANS "GOD, DO THIS FOR ME!"
"I AM" MEANS GOD-IN-ME AGREE!
"I AM" IS THE POWER OF GOD THROUGH ME!
"I AM" MEANS THE GOD-IN-ME AGREE!

Power of Words, Power of Thought, Power of Silence

In keeping the power of words in front of you, these two words, "I AM," are the most powerful two words anyone can say. I am … is the absolute principle of man; I am … is the God-part of the Soul that fulfills <u>and</u> provides for us every time we speak. "I am" is the source of our individuality, the source of our power. "I'm," "I" or "my" have the same intense power. Therefore, I am, is the way *we ask God for everything,* except most of the time we do it in a complete state of unawareness.

Instead, we are calling on God to give us pain, sickness, fatigue, lack and stress. We make up nicknames for ourselves and call for situations we would not like to experience, but have to, because of our power! We unconsciously connect dreadful, harmful words to our "I am." I say *unconscious* because in my experience, people *do not hear* most of what comes out of their mouths, especially when we are condemning ourselves.

We are extremely powerful beings. We can practice the power of our "I am" to prove it works or we can recall what we already have created and experienced.

To stop drama in my life, I spent days in silence. I was careful not to use Law against myself by getting involved in other people's drama, by speaking only when spoken to and by not engaging conversation with anyone.

Unconscious Self-Sabotage

When I can't,
When I'm trying,
If I want or I need;
I make it impossible
for me to succeed.

Power of Words, Power of Silence, Power of Thought

Please read "Unconscious Self-Sabotage" one more time. I ask you to read it twice, because when it first came through me I thought it was cute. So I read it, I sang it and it just would not leave my mind. I even printed it, framed it, and sat it up on an easel so I could see it. I went to bed with it on my mind and was awakened by an urge to find a dictionary. I realized in my sleep that I had no clear understanding of what the words *trying*, *need* and *want* really meant. I always thought I knew what they meant, but had never looked them up. To my dismay, *trying* means to subject oneself to strain, hardship or distress. The true meaning of *need* is a condition of lack, poverty, misfortune and obligation. *Want* means to fail, to be without, deficient, lack, destitution, deprived of and failure.

All I could think was I've been speaking these words all my life, thinking I knew the true meanings, but I didn't. I took this realization very personally. The way I saw my life was that I'd spent a lifetime asking for failure, lack and distress without knowing it. My first thought was about all the failed relationships I'd had and all the times we both "wanted and needed" each other and how those words sexually energized us and at the same time is the underlying reason why each relationship ended. It devastated me to know these words had sabotaged my life. The truth is, words are energy and become more powerful with intent and repetition.

My own life was proof enough for me that words, my words, really do have power. I decided right then to eliminate the words "want, need, try" from my vocabulary. Not an easy task. It took five years of constant self-observation, listening, keeping silent, choosing and exchanging words to finally succeed in waking myself up from what felt like a deep sleep.

The Power of Silence

I spent weekends in silence, communicating only if I had to through writing. I could hear the words repeating themselves in my thoughts. Through the *power of silence*, I observed how thoughts seemed to be running in and out of my mind without me initiating them, how I could not focus on one thought and how I couldn't even remember what I was thinking. I was out of control and knew it because I would even forget I was supposed to be silent and begin talking to whoever was around.

Staying silent takes real effort. Taking control of my thoughts was even harder. I repeated the act of being silent often because it became easier to control my thoughts when I was quiet. It was a lot easier to listen to myself and to what others were really saying. Not responding or not thinking of a response while another is talking increased my energy. I discovered that silence enhanced my power to observe others and myself more deeply than I knew possible. Silence is power. Ever notice how people will assume an answer for you when you do not respond to them in what they conceive of as a timely manner?

The Unconsciousness

I now understood that the first line in the 23rd Psalm, *"The Lord is my shepherd I shall not want,"* really means God is my guide, I shall not "fail." Had I known the meaning of those words long ago, would I have continued to call failure, lack and distress into my life? I'm not sure. It took two years after deciding to eliminate them for me to even hear myself consciously ask for failure, lack and distress and accept that I had said it … then change it. Again, it took two years or more for my Soul to begin the wake-up process.

Because of the Law of Cause and Effect and the power of the meaning of the words, *want*, *need* and *trying*, every Soul goes into a deep unawareness just hearing them. The job of the Soul is to give us what we ask for. When we ask for failure, lack and distress, we are asking the Soul for the "unnatural," which we do still receive. However, the power contained within those specific words sends the Soul into a state of unconsciousness, like sleepwalking.

How can we stop? We are constantly bombarded by these three words in every conversation, most songs, almost every book, rolling off everyone's tongue, on TV and on radio. Repetition keeps them embedded in our consciousness and in our unconsciousness throughout our lifetime. It's like an intended sabotage of the human Soul.

Prove this for yourself. Go to a library. Look up the words in a dictionary like an Oxford that is old enough to have original meanings with root words and language origins. Then think about the personal failures that have broken your heart, past relationships, experiences you thought would happen that didn't. Think about how deeply you *wanted* a certain thing, really letting its meaning, *failure...* sink into your understanding. Then *listen* to your friends and family ask for failure, lack and stress over and over, especially after you tell them what want, need and trying mean.

Everyone I have explained the words and their meanings to responds strangely. Each person starts by agreeing with me. Then something shifts in their brain and they *can't stop* saying want, need or trying, no matter what we talk about. The mind seems to get stuck like a scratched record or CD and people become unable to hear themselves or stop themselves from saying these words. I was quite distressed after watching people whom I considered extremely intelligent become unconscious and lose conscious control of their words and thoughts for varying amounts of time.

The experience is like watching an old "Twilight Zone" episode where three words put people into a deep sleep that gets deeper with every important activity that is *wanted or needed.* Since I kept getting such weird responses, I stopped sharing whatever I understood regarding those words at least until I was successful in eliminating them from my vocabulary, I thought. I discovered I could not eliminate them; I can only choose not to speak or think them. I am satisfied with my success of conscious choice and now it is my sincere desire that others will understand this information.

Casual Conversation

Casual conversation is unconscious, unkind conversation. Sometimes considered "small talk," casual conversation is usually mean, meaningless and occurs with someone we don't know and will most likely never see again. Some of us say the meanest things that friends would never hear us say. We rarely hear or recall these chats since they are often with people who mean nothing to us. We might find ourselves standing in a line when you or the person in front or behind you begin to talk. Or, you make eye contact with a person while you both witness a third person being rude or doing something to attract attention. Beware of chat you might have about it.

Casual conversation is always tainted with the ridicule, opinions and judgments that we would not express to loved ones or people we know. "Those words just slipped out without me thinking or hearing them" is what I would say. We are still responsible for them under Spiritual Law.

Casual conversation, when recalled, can remind us of work we still have to do regarding hidden resentments that remain within ourselves. In the evening while in a state of relaxation, conversations from earlier in the day can be recalled and forgiven.

PART THREE ————————

Thoughts, Ideas to Practice; More Thoughts,
Ideas to Consider

THE 'I' SONG

I AM, I CAN, I WILL, I MUST
I DESIRE, I WISH, I HAVE, I TRUST
I DECREE, I KNOW, I AM, I SEE
I CHOOSE, I MUST, I PREFER, I DECREE
I INTEND, I SHALL, I WILL, I WISH
I HAVE TO HAVE, I KNOW, I CHOOSE, I WISH
I DESERVE, I MUST HAVE, I DESIRE, I WILL
I CAN, I SEE, I KNOW, I WILL
I PREFER, I DECREE, I DESERVE, I SEE
I CHOOSE, I KNOW, I MUST HAVE, I DECREE
I INTEND, I DESIRE, I WILL, I KNOW, I CAN
I HAVE TO HAVE, I SHALL, I WISH, I COMMAND
I AM, I AM, I BELIEVE, I AM
I WILL, I DESIRE, I DESERVE, I DECREE
I INTEND, I MUST HAVE, I WILL, I KNOW, I SEE
I AM, I AM, I BELIEVE, I AM
I CAN, I WILL, I AM, I MUST
I DESIRE, I WISH, I HAVE, I TRUST
I SEE, I KNOW, I CHOOSE, I CAN
I SHALL, I WISH, I DECREE, I AM

Power of Words, Power of Repetition

'Considering the power of the words *"I am,"* the "I Song" is a powerful poem with the most positive, uplifting, simple words I could find to use as replacement words for the three that had sabotaged my life. The idea here is to keep the conscious mind overloaded with more positive, uplifting and empowering words in an attempt to retrain my mind to choose them first and automatically.

The 'I Song' came as the result of realizing how deeply embedded in my unconsciousness the words 'want, need, trying' were and how I couldn't stop myself from saying them even when I planned not to. Thinking ahead or forethought didn't work at all.

Knowing the power of repetition, I began by repeating the words of the "I Song" throughout my day to give my vocabulary several alternate choices. I hoped it would keep me from being at a loss when I was conscious enough to hear myself and change my words.

I put this poem on pocket-sized cards and kept them handy for the next two years. At first, I sounded strange to myself when saying, "I wish," "I desire" or "I have to have," but I didn't care, I was determined to succeed and I did.

THE 21-DAY MENTAL DIET

FOR THE NEXT 21 DAYS
I DECREE
ONLY POSITIVE WORDS
WILL COME FROM ME.

ALL THAT I SAY
MUST UPLIFT
EVERY PERSON, PLACE OR THING
I SEE.

IF I WEAKEN
AND START TO SLIP,
I'LL REMEMBER QUICKLY

To button my lip.

And from day-one
I'll begin again
Till control of my words
I regain.

Power of Repetition, Power of Words, Power of Silence

Some schools of thought claim it takes 21 days of repeating a phrase or statement for it to become part of our consciousness. The 21-Day Mental Diet is a personal listening exercise. It was hard to stop cursing, especially when there were certain curse words I was quite fond of and attached to.

Twenty-one days lasted a year or more because of my unconscious automatic cursing, which I did all the time. All those words I would not verbalize I would think of often. I didn't realize it at first, but thinking is equally as powerful. When I was awake enough to catch myself cursing, I'd switch to more positive words in my mind. Many times, I would forget, say something I know I didn't mean and have to start the 21–Day Mental Diet over repeatedly. Much of the "stuff" I said, I didn't hear until long after it was said.

Regular practice of the 21-Day Mental Diet helped me to stop reactions like yelling, cursing things, people or the situation before listening to reason. With lots of practice, I learned to take a breath first, then to count to 10 before mentally approaching anything. It really does take practice to slow the self down enough to listen, to think and learn to reply in a responsible manner.

A Simple Meditation

Sit up in a relaxed position
Feel your body breathe.
Give your mind a focus
Like the sun setting on the sea.
Tell each part to
Relax!
Starting with your feet
Take a deep breath, relax
But do not fall asleep.
Imagine you see each number
While your mind counts
One through four
Over and over for 15 minutes or more.
Plan each day to be
In the same place doing this -
In the same way.
Now, take a deep breath,
Open your eyes
And go about your day.

The Power of Meditation

For some, meditation is a form of prayer, devotion or a way to listen to God. For others, it has no spiritual value, it's just another way to relax, rejuvenate cells, energize the body and restore physical and emotional balance. A meditation can consist of movement as in dancing, walking or sitting quietly in silence. Meditation revives the inner Spirit or Soul as well as the physical body.

Traditionally, meditation means to ponder, to reflect or engage in contemplation or the act of concentration. The act of meditation is to direct one's thoughts, to be in control of one's thoughts, or to hold on to a particular thought for a given time. To meditate is to be conscious and mentally active.

The Simple Meditation directs you to take a few deep breaths inhaling and exhaling through the nose while sitting up, hands open and relaxed on your lap, feet flat on floor. Once the deep breaths relax you, start a mental visualization of the numbers 1, 2, 3 and 4 ... while silently counting to yourself. Repeat this for 5 to 20 minutes.

Once you're comfortable with the process, I suggest you replace counting with more empowering words like "health, wealth, love, success," which will have an even more positive effect on the emotions.

Once you begin to practice meditation, you'll realize, as I did, that it really requires focus. I did *not* have control of my thoughts and it is *not* easy to hold "one" thought. Please do not give up. Practice makes perfect. Meditating revitalizes the Soul, Spirit and Breath, gives the brain a rest and is like aerobics for the mind.

Holding onto one thought in meditation means to repeat the same numbers for up to 20 minutes. This simple act teaches the mind to concentrate. The side effects are the physical and spiritual body get energized, the body feels the relaxation of a 40-minute nap and muscles in the mind become stronger.

While meditation allows God to communicate directly to us, providing guidance and answering our question, it is not something we experience right away. It comes as a surprise after much practice, as will other benefits, which are personal.

WAKE-UP EVERYBODY!

WAKE UP EVERYBODY!
IT'S OUR WORDS WE MUST HEAR.

Our words have the power
To keep us in joy or in fear.
It's in those common words
We ALL say, "need, want and try."
These words keep us in
Failure, lack and distress.
That's their true meaning
And that's no lie!

Wake up all parents!
You're more important than you know.
Your words affect
Your children's self-image
As they grow.
Let's teach them to say
"I am, I can, I will, I know I deserve."
Tell them that life's experiences are created through
The power of their words.

The world will get much better
When it's self-empowerment we seek.
The world will change forever
When we change the way we
Think and speak.

Wake up all teachers!
Teach yourselves to understand
Each time you say "I" anything
You give your God-Self a command.
Teach each child that to achieve a goal
Is to be Aware of what they say.
Help them feel good about
Who they are, encourage them to reach
One goal per day.

THE WORLD WILL GET MUCH BETTER
WHEN IT'S SELF-EMPOWERMENT WE SEEK.
THE WORLD WILL CHANGE FOREVER
WHEN WE CHANGE THE WAY
WE THINK AND SPEAK.

WAKE UP EVERYBODY!
IN OUR WORDS LIES THE SOLUTION.
TO KNOW THE MEANING OF
EVERY WORD WE SAY
CREATES A PERSONAL SELF-EVOLUTION.

THE WORLD WILL TRULY GET BETTER
WHEN IT'S SELF-EMPOWERMENT WE SEEK.
YOUR WORLD WILL CHANGE FOREVER
WHEN YOU CHANGE THE WAY
YOU THINK AND SPEAK!

Power of Belief, Power of Words, Power of Thought

"Wake up Everybody" calls out to all people, asking them to awaken from the perpetual sleep created by Unconscious Self-Sabotage. **This sleep affects everyone who thinks, hears or speaks words that produce negative outcomes** like the words "want, need and trying." When we become alert, awake and aware of our God-given powers and how to use those skills, we can change how we experience our world.

My Awakening

First, I had to become conscious of hearing myself repeat those three words that as far as I was concerned had caused many negative experiences in my life. In an attempt to wake up, my cousin and best friend Denise and I agreed to snap our fingers whenever we heard the words "want, need or trying" pass each other's lips. Within two or three days, I accused Denise of mis-hearing me. I refused to believe I could be causing her to snap so much! She flat out accused me of lying. We found ourselves in a complete state of self-denial. Within a week, our fingers were too stiff to snap and then our hands became too sore and sensitive to clap. Soon this became emotional. We cried each time we heard the words or would be crying as we alerted each other.

We cried for the years of asking for failure, lack and stress in relationships, our health, business and finances. We cried mostly because no matter what we did, we could not stop ourselves from speaking the words "want, need or try." I was out of control. I could not stop those words from rolling off my tongue, no matter what I did. This showed me how deeply embedded in my consciousness or unconsciousness these words were. I released myself from any speaking activities until I could control my own thoughts and words. After months of concentrated repetition, the "I Song" finally began to pay off.

There was no time to think about anyone else's business because it requires real effort to change the way we think and speak. It is even harder to stop speaking words you don't say aloud, those we hear in our equally powerful thoughts. We began to practice chanting, "I am alert, awake and aware of my words, my thoughts." This made us hear each other even more.

I remember how happy we both were to be finally able to hear the words as soon as they left our mouths and change them right away. To be able to stop the words before speaking them was a monumental achievement. I discovered I had succeeded when I caught myself exchanging the words in my mind before speaking them. Oh my, what a happy day!

Living in the real world where all people are constantly asking for failure, lack and distress makes it easy to fall back into that zombie-like sleep. I remember that contagion can go either way. I find that if I say, "I wish, I desire, I must, I have to have," when I'm speaking, people automatically repeat my words exactly as I have said them.

THE BEST RELATIONSHIP

THERE'S A GUARDIAN INSIDE OF EVERYONE
WHO WILL GUIDE, GUARD AND PROTECT.
IT WILL FULFILL YOUR EVERY DESIRE
WHEN, WITH IT, YOU CONNECT.

YOUR FIRST MEETING MAY SEEM A BIT AWKWARD
SINCE YOU SHARE THE EXACT SAME SPACE.
BUT BY STANDING IN FRONT OF A MIRROR
YOU CAN MEET YOU FACE TO FACE.

EXAMINE YOUR SELF — SEE YOUR BEAUTY
AND ASK ANY QUESTION YOU LIKE.
LISTEN WITH YOUR HEART FOR THE ANSWER AND KNOW
YOUR SELF IS ALWAYS RIGHT.

TELL YOU "I LOVE YOU" OFTEN
AND LIKE MAGIC YOUR LIFE WILL SHIFT.
YOU WILL SOON REALIZE
THAT YOU AND YOUR-SELF ARE IN
THE BEST RELATIONSHIP.

Power of Intuition, Power of Silence

When we are comfortable with ourselves, when we trust our own ideas, thoughts and are confident with what we know and what we are doing, our physical body and our spiritual bodies are in alignment. This alignment is not constant, it appears, disappears and appears again as we evolve. We instinctively know that we have developed the best relationship because of our self-confidence, our complete trust in the Universe and in the self.

The Power of Intuition

Intuition is *knowing:* For some, it is knowing you have God or a guardian angel to guide, guard and protect you. Intuition is our God-given power to know. Sometimes God shows us things in our minds that either has happened or will happen. This used to be accepted as second sight or insight. Now it is known as sixth sense or psychic ability. Even though the ability is perfectly natural for every person, there are those who are afraid of it, call it evil or those who prefer you believe only certain people have this ability.

Intuitive Development

As a Spiritual life coach, I kept myself mentally, emotionally and spiritually attune by meditating before and after an in-person or telephone meeting with each client. This meant I was doing breathing exercises and meditating many times a day. I had plenty of energy and always felt good.

Life coaching is listening. Spiritual life coaching is listening, being aware of God working with and through each one, helping clients to accept, embrace and change their experiences. At the end of each meeting and because I always felt so good, I would remind each client to be on the lookout for something wonderful to happen this week, "just for you," I would add.

I started getting messages that said, "How did you know, I just got that promotion," "something wonderful did happen," "how'd you know?" I didn't know anything and didn't hold on to information shared during our sessions. Because of all the meditating and breathing, I believe I became an open vessel through which inspiration and intuition was used.

Intuition is one of our God-given powers that develops naturally as we practice meditation, silence, contemplation and deep-breathing exercises. Knowing becomes so natural that you don't know how you know things. They seem to come through you without effort. While I don't always know how I know things, I never reject or doubt any thoughts or ideas that appear during a session or meditation.

The one major discovery about my intuition that made it easier for me to accept is I have never been given wrong information about anything.

Sitting in silence helps in developing a deep trust in one's inner-self and in the thoughts and ideas that will appear.

THE FORGIVENESS LIST

I DID NOT WISH TO GIVE UP A THING
LET ALONE LEARN HOW TO FORGIVE.
THERE ARE MANY FOLKS I KNOW
I'LL NEVER SPEAK TO AGAIN
AS LONG AS I OR THEY LIVE.

WE ALL KNOW WHO "THEY" ARE.
THEY—ARE RESPONSIBLE FOR MY GRIEF.
I WOULDN'T EVEN BE MAKING A FORGIVENESS LIST,
EXCEPT, I HEARD DOING IT
GIVES MENTAL RELIEF.

RELUCTANTLY I WROTE
"FORGIVENESS LIST"
AND PUT MY NAME ON THE PAGE AT THE TOP.
I STARTED WRITING AND WRITING,
WRITING AND WRITING,
DIDN'T THINK I WOULD EVER STOP.

I WROTE ABOUT MY WHOLE LIFE

HAD I REALLY BEEN ANGRY THAT LONG?
I WAS ANGRY WITH MYSELF, MY FRIENDS,
FAMILY AND LOVERS. IT SHOCKED ME THAT
THOSE MEMORIES WERE STILL SO STRONG.
PEOPLE SHOWED UP IN MY DREAMS
I HADN'T THOUGHT ABOUT IN YEARS.
I'D WAKE UP AND PUT THEIR NAMES ON THE LIST
THEN, OTHER NAMES AND FACES WOULD APPEAR.

OH, I'M STILL UPSET WITH MANY OF THEM
JUST AS IF IT HAPPENED YESTERDAY.
BUT THIS LIST MADE ANGER EASY TO GIVE UP
AND KEPT ME FROM GIVING MORE OF
MY POWER AWAY.
FORGIVING LIKE THIS HAS TRULY CHANGED MY LIFE.
I ENCOURAGE ALL TO MAKE A FORGIVENESS LIST.
IT'S OPENED MY HEART AND MADE MORE SPACE
FOR PEACE AND LOVE TO EXIST.

IT WILL OPEN YOUR HEART
AND CREATE MORE SPACE
FOR PEACE AND LOVE TO EXIST.

The Power of Forgiveness

To forgive means to give up the energy of anger. Isn't it strange how hard it is to let that anger go. Ever noticed that the more angry you are, the more drained you feel after the anger is gone. It's like that because anger empowers the person or the thing you're angry with, not you. You are giving power away when you waste it on anger, hate, resentment, fear and jealousy.

Forgiveness changes the energy, opens the heart and opens doorways to new experiences. Forgiveness is another of our God-given powers we don't use enough! When we learn to forgive ourselves, the experience or situation and those who have been our perpetrators or our victims, we will truly understand freedom.

It's wonderful to feel nothing when, in the past, the energy between that person and me was thick and negative. Once I placed names on my forgiveness list, I would read out loud that I fully and freely forgive each name on the list. After forgiving in this manner and then meeting the people listed, the energy between us seems new, easy and effortless. The best part is we do not have to forgive in a face-to-face manner; we can write it or speak it aloud during alone time. In cases where I refused to forgive, a heavy energy remains between that person and me. We are unable to speak or stay in the same environment. For those betrayers who were good friends, I have had to put them on my forgiveness list more than 10 times or even more, until I'm over it. When writing a name on my list suddenly seems ridiculous, I'm over it. The process really cleanses and changes the energy between you and others and is a great beginning to creating the habit of forgiveness.

The Importance of Forgiving

The truth about forgiveness is we should be repeating "I forgive myself" more than 1,000 times a day, starting upon awakening simply because we are all prone to unconscious behavior as well as unconscious thoughts.

I made the discovery about myself just hanging out with a friend in her condominium community. As we were sitting and talking, my friend suggested that we visit an empty condo to check out the layout. I entered through the door after she entered by open window. There were things left in the home like food, clothes and shoes, that we took. She even went back in without me to get the things she had divided for herself and put stuff in a pile for me. Somehow, I couldn't find the time to go back and then she called me whispering over the phone that the owners were in their condo. That's when I realized my "unconsciousness," I then mentally recalled I had taken part in a burglary, a break-in. The next morning I bagged everything I had taken and without being seen by my friend or anyone, I returned the items to the owner's balcony and covered them with a sheet. I haven't stopped forgiving myself. In fact, catching myself stealing really hurt me, so yes, I forgive myself as often as I can.

Knowing the Law, I could only get upset with *myself.* I never shared that I returned the stuff I had stolen with my friend. She takes things from her job all the time and would never understand that what we did was stealing. Falling back into that deep unconscious self-sabotage (zombie) sleep that I referred to earlier is so easy. When all I had to say was, "no, that's stealing."

There are other times we must keep ourselves conscious like when we are driving to keep from calling out obscenities to challenged drivers without thinking. In restaurants where we might steal packs of cream or sugar. While watching TV or when we think and whisper nasty things "under our breath" so to speak. There is always more than one reason to forgive ourselves.

THE LITTLE CAN

WHEN BOMBARDED WITH NEGATIVITY
FROM THE MOUTH OF MY FELLOW MAN,
I RESORT TO MY IMAGINATION
AND UNDER HIS CHIN
I PLACE A LITTLE CAN.

I HANG IT FROM BOTH HIS EARS
WITH GREAT BIG CHAINS OF STEEL
STRONG ENOUGH TO HOLD THOSE WORDS

AND THE LITTLE CAN PERFECTLY STILL.
WHILE HE SPEAKS,
I MAKE SURE HIS WORDS
ARE FALLING IN THE LITTLE CAN.
THEN—IN MY MIND,
I LIGHT A MATCH
AND FLICK
IT'S IN AT MY COMMAND.

I CHEER AS THE FLAMES CONSUME THOSE WORDS
THAT COULD HAVE HURT BOTH HIM AND ME.
WHEN HE'S FINISHED,
I REMOVE MY GEAR
AND RETURN TO REALITY.

Power of Imagination, Power of Silence

This exercise was created to encourage one to use the power of imagination instead of words that could easily cause misunderstandings.

Most people do not hear themselves using negative expressions, calling forth illness like cancer, Alzheimer's or arthritis, saying negative things about themselves, calling themselves old, sick or other names and it is impolite to ask them to be quiet.

Whenever I practice mentally placing a little can under someone's mouth and burning their words while they speak, my imagination makes them look so funny that it stops me from hearing or remembering what they were saying in the first place. That is an example of the power of imagination and thought. Imagination is another of our God-given powers. We don't have to believe in it. We should at least explore it.

A way to explore it is to sit quietly, giving attention to your breathing for up to three minutes. Use that time to think about an experience you would like, or a trip or some other scenario. Then, in your mind, create the experience, or take the trip, filling in details. Practice daily for about 21 days, then stop and allow the Universe time to respond to you.

PEACE

IF PEACE COULD BE MADE TANGIBLE
I'D TURN IT INTO A SPRAY.
I'D SWEETEN IT, BOTTLE AND GIFT-WRAP IT
THEN I'D GIVE IT ALL AWAY.

I'D MAKE IT SO THAT
ONE SPRAY ELIMINATES ANGER,
TWO SPRAYS RELIEVE PAIN.
THREE SPRAYS SAVE US THE ENERGY AND TIME
WE WASTE ON BLAME AND SHAME.

IF PEACE COULD BE MADE TANGIBLE
I'D BREW IT EVERY DAY.
I'D STORE IT IN LARGE QUANTITIES
JUST TO GIVE IT ALL AWAY.

I'D LABEL EACH BOTTLE "DANGEROUS"
FOLLOW DIRECTIONS PLEASE!
OVER-SPRAYING WILL LEAD TO LOVE AND JOY
AND WILL PUT YOUR MIND AT EASE.

OH, IF PEACE COULD BE MADE TANGIBLE
I'D TURN IT RIGHT INTO A SPRAY
AND UNTIL THE WORLD BECOMES PEACEFUL,
I'LL KEEP ON GIVING IT AWAY.
IT'S ABOUT PEACE!

Power of Imagination, Power of Thought, Power of Words

This is another example of using our power of imagination to engage our minds in giving peace a sense of taste and smell.

About Peace

Peace is an inner-calm so complete that nothing can disturb it. Jesus knew without doubt that God is All and in All. This gave Him the peace that *passeth* all understanding, the true peace of God.

Peace is not listed as a God-given power because peace is all the powers of God combined. Living without day-to-day drama, no anger, no sadness, no disagreements, no disturbances or threats of disharmony of any kind, not even by surprise, is the meaning of living in peace. Peace is displayed in character, through confidence, intuition, imagination, belief, joy and trust.

The Power of Imagination

Imagination is the power of the mind to form images or concepts of things not yet present to the senses or within the actual experience of the person involved. When used with intention, the imagination is referred to as a creative power.

It's phrases like "It was just my imagination playing tricks on me" that keeps everyone believing their power of imagination is a joke, setting up doubt and disbelief. The truth is that all the great and wonderful things that exist in our world had their beginnings in someone's imagination. Our creative process begins in our imagination. Our creative imaginings can be used to improve upon something that already exists, or to bring new things into existence.

You'll have to prove this to yourself. Just understand that whatever you imagine, visualize or hold in your mind is what shows up in your life.

Test your power of imagination by choosing a desire or goal you wish to experience. If you can say it and see it in one word like love, success, health or wealth, then do so. Now, use your imagination to see your goal fulfilled. Imagine the completion of that one goal. Hold the images of the end result in your mind for a minute or more, then let them go. Repeat the process often.

Imagination gets stronger with each visual repetition of your creation. Allow yourself to become an observer as your imagination continues the imaging process for and through you. Be sure you really desire what you imagine since what we imagine often manifests into reality. Keep practicing until your vision becomes a real experience.

HOW TO MEET YOUR HIGHER SELF

MAKE NO EXCUSE FOR ANYTHING
LISTEN TO YOURSELF TALK
KEEP OPINIONS TO YOURSELF
MAKE THE BEST OF EVERY SITUATION
LEARN TO BE IN THE HERE AND NOW
ALWAYS HAVE GOALS
TAKE RESPONSIBILITY FOR YOUR ACTIONS
STAND FOR WHAT YOU BELIEVE
KNOW THAT JOY IS YOUR BIRTHRIGHT
BE YOUR OWN BEST FRIEND
USE FREE WILL WISELY
NEVER LIE AGAIN
REFUSE TO THINK LIKE A VICTIM
FILL YOUR MIND WITH PEACE
FEED YOURSELF CONFIDENCE
BE WILLING TO SUCCEED

SAY "I LOVE YOU" IN THE MIRROR
TREAT EVERYONE WITH RESPECT
PAY ATTENTION TO DETAILS
AND YOU WILL GET WHAT YOU EXPECT
YOU WILL MEET YOUR HIGHER SELF.

Power of Thought, Power of Words, Power of Belief, Power of Silence, Power of Imagination, Power of Intuition, Power of Repetition

Living by the rules within this poem is one way to meet your real self, to change your environment or change your life offering a shift in consciousness.

Whenever we begin to take responsibility for our actions and become aware of our thoughts and what we say, a change has been initiated within you that affects others. You may hear discouraging opinions from friends and family regarding the new you. Negative opinions from others usually mean you are doing something great for yourself. As you become confident, you may be labeled, "cocky" or a "know-it-all" depending on your attitude.

You will waste precious time and energy if you feel you have to defend yourself in any way. Paying attention to details in your life and taking time to record and read your goals will deliver you from gossip, casual conversation and unconscious self-sabotage.

TEST THAT POWER

IF THERE'S THAT MUCH POWER IN OUR WORDS
I'LL CHANGE MY ENTIRE NAME
RICH, BEAUTIFUL, BLISSFUL ROBERTS
IS NOW MY CLAIM TO FAME.

I LIKE THE FACT THAT I'M CALLING ME

What I intend to be.
So I'll keep this name until I see
That power in our word is the key.

Since there's so much power in our words
Let's make a blissful, rich, beauty appear
Call me, come on, let's test that power
We can do this with nothing to fear.
Ready?

Rich, beautiful, blissful Roberts
Oh yes! I like the sound of that name.
Rich, beautiful, blissful Roberts
This name is my claim to fame.

Rich, beautiful, blissful Roberts
This time use your own last name.
Rich, beautiful, blissful Who?
See, now it's your claim to fame.

Rich, beautiful, blissful Who?
Your life will never be the same.
Cause you're now
Rich, beautiful, blissful Who?
Ok! Ok! Ok!

Power of Words, Power of Thought, Power of Belief, Power of Imagination, Power of Repetition

"Test That Power" is a fun way to use Law while combining your powers of words, thought, belief, imagination and repetition all at once.

The Power of Thought

Our power of thought is the most productive and creative of our God-given powers. Thought power is evidenced continually throughout our entire lifetime. The phrase "As a man thinketh in his heart so is he" means that it's not what we wish and pray for, but that which we keep hidden in our mind, heart and Soul do we receive and become.

We may not believe it but everything we do springs from our hidden seeds of thought and could not have appeared without them. Each person, while nearly always unconscious or unaware is literally a combination of character and what he or she thinks.

Those acts we call "spontaneous" and "unpremeditated" come from the same hidden seeds of thought.

Basically, good thoughts and actions can never produce bad results. Bad thoughts and actions can never produce good results. A particular train of thought persisted in, be it good or bad, cannot fail to produce its results on the character, the life and circumstances of the thinker.

Thinking

True thinking is to apprehend and employ thought consciously and with purpose. All achievements, whether in the business, intellectual or spiritual world, are the result of consciously directed thought.

Consciously directed thought, as in meditation, contemplation or concentration, is an act of will- power allowing one to think with purpose expecting fulfillment or accomplishment.

We soon find that as we alter our thoughts toward things and other people, things and other people will alter their actions toward us.

It's a real error to imagine that thought can be kept secret. It cannot. Thought quickly crystallizes into habit and habit solidifies into circumstances we may not immediately notice. Once discovered, the only way to change a circumstance is to change one's thought. All successful circumstantial changes are achieved through careful watchfulness and awareness of thought.

KEEP ON LIVING

IF WE KEEP ON LIVING
WE'LL DISCOVER
THAT THE WORD "NEVER"
DOES NOT EXIST.
ANGELS LIVE AMONG US.
DISEASE IS MORE
THAN JUST AN ILLNESS,
AND EVERYTHING IS CAUSE AND EFFECT.
IF WE KEEP ON LIVING,
WE'LL DISCOVER
THAT EVERYONE LIES.
EVERY ENCOUNTER IS A LESSON
AND A BLESSING.
EVIL IS AN ALTERED EXPRESSION OF GOOD.
NOTHING IS MORE SATISFYING
THAN ACHIEVING PERSONAL GOALS.
WE KEEP GROWING UP TO OURSELVES.
IF WE JUST KEEP ON LIVING
WE WILL DISCOVER
THAT THE GREATEST POWER IN LIFE
IS LOVE.

Power of Thought, Power of Belief, Power of Intuition

If we keep on living, we discover that love is life! Love is also called God. Loving is caring while accepting the things about others and ourselves we cannot change.

It is well known that ***everyone lies.*** In today's world when it is revealed that a person has lied, they quickly claim, "I mis spoke." To clear up any misunderstanding, to misspeak is to lie, to intentionally deceive is to tell an untruth.

While there are many different kinds and levels of lies, we hear lies and we learn lying from the womb. Children are taught to lie for parents, from parents early in life. Lying becomes a habit that quickly turns into an automatic function of the mind. As this happens, we then automatically lie about most things consciously and unconsciously.

While some people just like to lie, others lie to control, to protect or hurt. To stop or even minimize our habitual lying requires much more discipline than most of us are ready to exert because it's similar to drug abuse. Like drug abuse, habitual lying is very hard to change or eliminate.

Lying confuses the Soul of the liar. The Soul's job is to attract to you and provide for you everything you think, say and intend. Lying is a misuse of the power of words, the power of thought, the power of imagination and a general misuse of divine Law. Once again, the Soul can only give you what you say, think and believe. While the Soul does not distinguish lies from truth, it is connected to and governed by Law.

Behind every lie is a reason or motive that grew out of good, love, greed, jealousy, resentment or fear. Law must balance all things. So lies will be told to you with the same energy you attached to those you told. Consequently, every lie gets revealed.

Many of us eventually discover that everything we say and do really does in some way come back to us. So, it really does matter that we do what we love and that we love our life and our existence.

I WILL

I WILL PROVE TO MYSELF THAT I LOVE ME
IN EVERY WAY I CAN.
I WILL GIVE ME MY ATTENTION FIRST.
I WILL TELL ME HOW SPECIAL I AM.
I WILL TAKE MYSELF TO FUN PLACES.
I WILL KEEP MY BODY CLEAN.
I WILL SING LOVE SONGS TO MYSELF ALL DAY
TO BOOST MY SELF-ESTEEM.

I WILL ADORN MYSELF IN MY MIRRORS
TILL I LOOK AND FEEL MY BEST.
I WILL TELL ME HOW IMPORTANT I AM.
I WILL COMMAND HEALTH, WEALTH, LOVE AND SUCCESS.

I WILL DO THOSE THINGS THAT BRING ME JOY.
I WILL LOVE EVERYTHING I DO.
I WILL SAY "I LOVE ME" TO MYSELF
TILL MY LIFE SHOWS ME THAT IT'S TRUE.

I WILL PROVE TO MYSELF THAT I LOVE ME
IN EVERY WAY I CAN.
I WILL GIVE ME MY ATTENTION FIRST
TO REMIND ME OF HOW SPECIAL I AM.

Power of Thought, Power of Forgiveness, Power of Imagination, Power of Intuition

As we evolve, we realize how separated from the belief in God and self we are. The separation makes us forget that love, health, joy, success and happiness are the real reasons we exist and should be natural experiences.

However, we go on for years without ever thinking about ourselves, loving ourselves, or our bodies. Our self-esteem gets so sensitized to negativity, self-hatred seems normal. Then, we start announcing how sick we are of this or that, we start agreeing with and listening to the negativity of our co-workers, friends and relatives. Telling ourselves about love or even thinking about proving our love for ourselves is a rare, unheard-of experience. In fact, we sometimes hate ourselves so much, we feel silly and think we sound dumb saying "I love me" instead of feeling empowered.

Loving ourselves unconditionally is probably our most difficult life task. My teacher and friend, Rev. Alma told all the students in her Science of Mind classes to say, "I love myself," 5,000 times a day. No one could do it. At the time, no one had the kind of stamina it takes to repeat the same phrase for 10 minutes. Saying it 5,000 times would take more than an hour. What Rev. Alma didn't tell her students was that those who succeeded in chanting "I love myself" an hour or more each day for three weeks will begin to experience love from the Universe in strange, surprising and unusual ways. If one continues the practice, everything in your life begins to fall perfectly in place. You will experience love in the form of acceptance, caring, assurance and surprise coming from co-workers, peers, family, friends and strangers.

"I Will" serves as a promise to the self as well as a reminder that loving the self is the most important gift one can give. As we realize that our bodies will respond favorably when we talk to ourselves, chanting things like love, health, joy, success, prosperity and more, we can test our powers of words, thought, imagination and repetition.

REPETITION

HOW DO YOU FORM A BELIEF?
REPETITION
HOW DO YOU BELIEVE A BELIEF?
REPETITION
HOW DO YOU KEEP A BELIEF?
REPETITION
HOW DO YOU KNOW WHAT YOU BELIEVE?
REPETITION
HOW ARE YOU MADE TO BELIEVE?
REPETITION
HOW ARE YOU TRAINED TO BELIEVE?
REPETITION
HOW DO YOU CHANGE A BELIEF?
REPETITION
HOW WILL I CHANGE MY BELIEFS?
REPETITION

Power of Words, Power of Belief

Everything we have learned, everything we have accomplished has been because we have combined our powers of thought, words, belief and more with our power of repetition.

Power of Repetition

Repetition goes on around the world continuously and constantly. Things are repeated all the time. We even repeat ourselves. Nothing is more powerful than our power of repetition. Because of its simplicity and repeated use, repetition goes unrecognized as a God-given power.

We can think of the power of repetition as the power of persistence to help grasp a portion of its meaning. Repetition works like an unstoppable generator energizing words, thoughts, imagination or meditation until it takes on form. Repetition is required for success in everything. Repetition is how we train, retrain, learn or unlearn all things. Repetition results in demonstration.

We can easily become aware of the words we are repeating by taking an *honest* look at our life and all we are experiencing.

Listen to people repeat things, pay attention to the things they ask for over and over without hearing themselves. Learn to listen to yourself, understand your power of repetition and use it to your advantage.

PART FOUR ————————————

*Practical Single-Mindedness; Self–Empowerment
Ideas, Thoughts*

KEEP IT SIMPLE, SPIRIT

KEEP IT SIMPLE, SPIRIT
JUST CALL EVERYTHING GOD.
GOD IS ALL SHAPES, ALL FACES
AND IN EVERYTHING,
EVEN IN THE STUFF THAT'S STRANGE AND ODD.
DOESN'T MATTER WHAT IT DOES
OR WHO IT TRIES TO BE,
YOU JUST KEEP IT SIMPLE, SPIRIT.
CALL IT ALL GOD.
AND GOD, YOU WILL SEE.

Power of Belief, Power of Thought, Power of Words

"Keep It Simple, Spirit" is equivalent to the idea in the Bible about *keeping a single eye.* Calling every person and thing "God" is exactly the kind of thing that can eventually change one's perspective.

Recognizing everyone or thing as God or good eliminates the belief in or the worship of more than one energy. Calling God or good continues the idea that this world, man, everything in it, above it and around it belongs to God or is God in expression.

When I practice silently saying to everyone and everything "The God in me greets the God in you," attitudes change instantly, anger vanishes and challenges become easier to overcome. While it seems magical, it's proof that we can change energy rather quickly using the power of thought.

CONSCIOUS AWARENESS

CONSCIOUS AWARENESS, CONSCIOUS AWARENESS.
I BREATHE IN THE AIR OF GOD.
I SEE THROUGH THE EYES OF GOD.
I HEAR THROUGH THE EARS OF GOD.
I SPEAK WITH THE VOICE OF GOD.
MY THOUGHTS ARE FROM GOD ABOUT GOD.
I AM TOTALLY ANIMATED BY GOD.
ALL THAT I AM IS GOD-MEETING-GOD
WITHIN THE KINGDOM OF GOD.

CONSCIOUS AWARENESS, CONSCIOUS AWARENESS.
WE BREATHE IN THE AIR OF GOD.
WE SEE THROUGH THE EYES OF GOD.
WE HEAR THROUGH THE EARS OF GOD.
WE SPEAK WITH THE VOICE OF GOD.
OUR THOUGHTS ARE FROM GOD ABOUT GOD.
WE ARE TOTALLY ANIMATED BY GOD.
ALL THAT WE ARE IS GOD-MEETING-GOD
WITHIN THE KINGDOM OF GOD.
ALL THAT YOU ARE IS GOD-MEETING-GOD
WITHIN THE KINGDOM OF GOD.

Power of Thought, Power of Belief, Power of Imagination

"Conscious Awareness" is about our powers of words, thought, belief and imagination and how they affect our perspective. Here again, acknowledging God, knowing that we live always in the presence of and in the Kingdom of God is a basic truth containing enormous power.

Acknowledgement of joy, peace, love and happiness cause them to become a natural part of our consciousness.

Many of us actually think *and* believe that our thoughts, words and actions are independent of God. This makes maintaining conscious awareness seem unattainable, impossible and totally unrealistic.

Believing that God *is* All, and *in* All, is the basic prayer of acknowledgment required to live the promise of joy and salvation. The Soul already knows what we desire, what we require and what we're dreaming, since all desires are placed in us *by* God.

Our job is to embrace and acknowledge God as all the presence, all the power and all the knowledge there is in each one of us and in the Universe to experience everything we desire in peace.

To all those who can maintain and achieve the continuous thought that God *is* All and *in* All, the promise is before you can think or speak the thought, your desire is fulfilled.

MY PERSONAL CREDO

I AM MADE IN THE IMAGE AND LIKENESS OF GOD,
EXPRESSING EXACTLY AS I AM.
I AM SPIRIT, I AM DIVINE,
I AM AN OFFSPRING OF PURE INTELLIGENCE.
I AM CAPABLE. I NOW BRING FORTH INTO MY WORLD ALL THE GREATNESS
THERE IS IN ME.
SPIRIT INSTRUCTS ME IN WAYS TO EXPRESS MY LOVE,
IN UNIVERSAL FORM OVERFLOWING ALL PEOPLE, ALL PLACES, ALL THINGS.
I LOVE MYSELF, I HONOR MYSELF, I PRAISE MYSELF, I BLESS MYSELF.

I HAVE A MAGNETIC IRRESISTIBLE QUALITY.
I AM A MAGNET OF BLISS. I AM A MAGNET OF JOY. I RADIATE
DIVINE LOVE.
HUMANITY LOVES TO BASK IN THE RADIANT LIGHT OF MY
PRESENCE.
MY VALUE IS HIGH. THERE IS A MARKET FOR ME
EVERYWHERE.
MY PROSPERITY NOW OVERFLOWS IN GENEROUS SERVICE TO
ALL.
MY SUCCESS DRAWS FORTH SUCCESSES.
MY TALENT IS NOW UNCOVERED AND IS NOW APPRECIATED
IN SERVICE,
BRINGING ME RICH, FINANCIAL REWARDS.
MY INGENUITY AND POWER OF INVENTION ARE NOW IN THE
FOREFRONT AND I SERVE HUMANITY.
I AM INVALUABLE TO HUMANITY.
I GENEROUSLY PRAISE, ENCOURAGE AND UPLIFT ALL WHO I
MEET.
MY ENERGY MAKES OTHERS ENERGIZED.
MY GENEROSITY MAKES OTHERS GENEROUS.
I AM A SEED PLANTED IN THE SOIL OF RICHES, GROWING ALL
THAT PROSPERS ME UNTO ME.
I FLOURISH LIKE A TREE PLANTED BY THE RIVERS OF WATER,
GROWING EFFORTLESSLY IN HEALTH, BEAUTY, POWER AND
LIFE.
I AM UNDER DIVINE LAW. I BRING FORTH FRUIT IN MY
SEASON.

DIVINE LAW SERVES AND BLESSES ME AS I SERVE AND BLESS
MYSELF.
I AM AWARE OF MY HIGHER-SELF, THE GOD I AM, THE ONE
IN WHOM I LIVE, MOVE AND HAVE MY BEING AS THE ONLY
UNLIMITED SOURCE OF MY UNLIMITED SUPPLY OF
ABUNDANCE.

I LOVE MYSELF, I HONOR MYSELF, I PRAISE MYSELF, I BLESS MYSELF.
I HAVE SELF-RESPECT, I HOLD MY HEAD UP HIGH, I AM POISED, I AM ERECT WITH A FIRM STEP.
I AM EXCITED OVER THE SUCCESSES OF OTHERS, I REJOICE ALWAYS IN THE PROSPERITY OF ALL, AND I BLESS ALL.
I RADIATE THE ENERGY OF DIVINE EXPRESSION.
MY BUSINESS IS TO LOVE, TO COMMUNICATE LOVE AND TO LOVE ALL UNCONDITIONALLY.
I AM AN EVER-FLOWING FOUNTAIN OF RESOURCEFULNESS, CONNECTED TO THE FOUNTAINHEAD WITHIN ME.
I LOVE AND I BLESS ALL PERSONS, ALL SITUATIONS, ALL THINGS, ALWAYS.

I AM THE POWER OF DIVINE EXPRESSION, NOW TRANSLATING DIVINE INVISIBLE SUBSTANCE INTO TANGIBLE VISIBLE FORM.
MY FAITH IS UNLIMITED, BASED IN KNOWLEDGE, TRUTH, TRUST AND REASON.
I AM, I CAN, I HAVE ALL THINGS BECAUSE OF THIS DIVINE POWER IN ME.
DIVINE WISDOM GUIDES ME, I AM ALWAYS SECURE WITHIN AS I UTILIZE MY TIME, MY SUBSTANCE, MY LIFE TO MY GREATEST BENEFIT.
I AM JOYOUS, I AM JOY-FILLED, I AM BLISSFUL, I AM FULFILLED.

DIVINE INTELLIGENCE KEEPS ME CONSCIOUS OF MY WORDS, MY INTENTIONS AND MY THOUGHTS.
DIVINE INSPIRATION ALLOWS ME TO EXPRESS MYSELF IN PEACE WITH WISDOM.
I TRUST, I BELIEVE, I HAVE FAITH IN MY HIGHER-SELF, THE ALMIGHTY ONE WITHIN ME BLESSING AND PROSPERING ME.
I AM A LAMB TO MY HIGHER-SELF. AS MY GUARDIAN ANGEL, MY HIGHER-SELF GUIDES, DIRECTS AND INFLUENCES ME IN WAYS THAT SERVE ME.

I KEEP A HIGH WATCH UPON THE WORDS OF MY MOUTH AND
THE MEDITATIONS OF MY HEART.
I AM TRUE TO MYSELF AND MY TRUTHFULNESS DEFENDS ME.
CONFIDENTLY AND RECEPTIVELY I LISTEN AND FOLLOW THAT
GUIDANCE FROM WITHIN.
THE POWER OF MY HIGHER-SELF FILLS MY WHOLE BEING, MY
WHOLE LIFE.
THE JOY OF FULFILLMENT FILLS AND COVERS ALL THAT IS
MINE, ALL THAT I PUT MY HANDS TO PROSPER.

THE POWER OF DEMONSTRATION IS NOW MINE.
ALL MY GOALS AND DESIRES NOW MATERIALIZE AND ARE NOW
DEMONSTRATED IN MY EXPERIENCE.
I NOW MOVE IN THE FLOW AND WITH THE FLOW OF MY LIFE.
I KNOW MY HIGHER-SELF KNOWS ABSOLUTELY EVERYTHING
AND NOW TELLS ME AND SHOWS ME EXACTLY WHAT TO DO,
HOW TO DO IT, WHEN TO DO IT, IN THE PERFECT WAY, AT
THE PERFECT TIME FOR EVERY SITUATION IN MY LIFE!

YES, YES, YES. LOVE, JOY, PEACE, WISDOM, POWER, BEAUTY,
LIFE
FOLLOWS ME NOW AND ALL THE DAYS OF MY LIFE AS I DWELL
IN DIVINE LOVE, ABIDING IN DIVINE LAW AND TRUTH NOW,
TODAY, FOREVER.
SO IT IS!

Power of Thought, Power of Words, Power of Belief, Power of Forgiveness, Power of Meditation, Power of Imagination, Power of Intuition, Power of Repetition, Power of Silence

"My Personal Credo" acknowledges who, what, where, why, when, how and so what, as it refers to the Spiritual Being.

Patience

The more spiritually developed I think I've become, the more I must stay focused on patience with my fellow man and myself. I've experienced times when I have no tolerance for people, for my time being infringed upon or my energy wasted. These misguided thoughts occur when we think we have grown or have a highly developed spirituality. Thinking one can be more spiritually linked than another or that we must develop our spirituality is not true. Some think that spirituality is something we must strive for. We don't because we are naturally spiritual, we are spiritual beings. No achieving, developing, training or higher mindedness required. The only requirement is understanding.

When these mis-thoughts happen, I have to give more time to myself in prayer, thanksgiving, humbleness and forgiveness to create the energy of patience. I can do all of the above by taking time to read the Credo. It only takes six minutes to read. Its energy lasts all day. It serves as an all-empowering daily affirmation that energizes the body, revitalizes the mind, stimulates and uplifts the Soul instantly while keeping one on a healthy spiritual track throughout the day. Prove it to yourself.

FEELS SO GOOD

THIS IS THE BEST TIME OF MY LIFE.
IT FEELS SO GOOD TO BE FREE.
I'M FREE OF REGRETS AND EXPECTATIONS,
I'VE DISCOVERED REALITY.

MY PERCEPTIONS, PLUS MY OPINIONS
CREATE ILLUSIONS FOR MY DAY.
I HAVE MERELY TO CHANGE MY THOUGHTS
TO MAKE MY LIFE LOOK A DIFFERENT WAY.

I'M HAVING THE BEST TIME OF MY LIFE,
NO JUDGMENTS TO FALL BACK ON.
HOW LIFE IS — IS JUST HOW I SEE IT
WITHOUT CALLING IT RIGHT OR WRONG.
FROM THE KNOWN INTO THE UNKNOWN,
TO POSSIBILITIES WITHOUT LIMITATIONS.
I CHOOSE TO LIVE IN THE NOW OF MY LIFE
WITHOUT THE CAMOUFLAGE OF PAST SITUATIONS.

I'VE GOT NO LIKES OR DISLIKES,
I LOVE EVERYTHING I SEE.
RIGHT NOW IS THE BEST TIME OF MY LIFE,
IT FEELS SO GOOD TO BE FREE.

RIGHT NOW IS THE BEST TIME OF MY LIFE,
IT FEELS SO GOOD TO BE ME!

Power of Thought, Power of Words, Power of Belief

Consider this: As each Soul practices acknowledging the presence, the power and the knowledge of God, he or she will create a more joyous, prosperous and peaceful life. Practice guarantees a sort of Soul security. Just acknowledging God is a powerful tool of preservation and salvation.

All that I have asked you to consider I am also doing. I started by paying attention to my "I am," adding uplifting words like I am rich, I am well, I am healthy and I am happy, just to name a few.

I chanted *so* often because when I started, I didn't believe any of what I was saying! It felt like I was lying. For the same reason I could not sit quietly while chanting, I was more comfortable walking, driving or cooking. However, after chanting every day as often as I could remember for two months, I was finally able to chant silently while sitting comfortably.

In just a few months of consistency, repetition began to reinforce things. I didn't have to force myself to chant or to remember what I was chanting. I became more peaceful. Patience with myself and others became easier. My level of confidence increased to the point that I didn't have to chant so often. I know that I'm a spiritual being living in a Spiritual Universe where I'm having one spiritual or Soulful experience after another.

Now I'm down to a simple chant of single words like health, wealth, love, success. The more I believe in my powers of words, meditation, imagination, silence and repetition, the more I am in control of my life. Therefore, fulfillment is guaranteed.

Utilizing your God-given powers is a way to guarantee fulfillment. Our *power of meditation* allows us to combine our powers thereby increasing our effectiveness.

BLISS BALLING

Bliss Balling uses your powers of meditation, silence, imagination, thought, word, repetition and belief. While you will not consciously use your powers of intuition and forgiveness, each will be greatly enhanced by the process since Bliss Balling conserves and restores energy.

The simple acts of meditation and breathing activates the power of intuition. Forgiveness is easier when you are tending your desires. The process takes about five minutes once memorized.

Directions: set aside 15 minutes where you will not be disturbed. There are four visualizations. Choose one and practice for at least 30 days. Read entire meditation through several times to familiarize yourself with the process. Practice with an open book until memorized. Please do not think you can shortcut the process by not doing the relaxation. For each visualization: Always start with relaxation, follow the process through to "As the mist clears," the beginning of each visualization for health, love, money or success. Remember, you are working with your subconscious mind, so be patient with yourself.

Each step is important and should not be skipped. Practice as often as you like until early evening. This meditation will energize your mind and body and may keep you awake if done late in the evening.

Meditation: "Bliss Balling" - Relaxation

Sit up comfortably straight, feet flat on floor, hands open on lap, eyes closed.

Gently take a deep breath through the nostrils, imagine the breath traveling through-out the body, hold the breath at the top of head, release the breath, exhale through the nostrils.

Take 3-4 breaths like this, then breathe normally.

Bring your attention to your scalp, imagine you feel your scalp relaxing, feel it relax.

Focus your attention on your forehead, relax your forehead.

Imagine you see your eyelids. Now, feel your eyelids relax.

Imagine you can feel your cheeks and jawbone, feel your cheeks and jawbone relax.

Think about your throat and back of neck, feel your throat, feel the back of your neck as you relax.

Imagine energy flowing through your shoulders, arms and hands. The energy relaxes your shoulders, arms and hands.

Bring your attention to your chest, feel your chest area rise and fall as you breathe. Each breath relaxes your chest.

Become aware of your solar plexus and the small of your back – allow them to relax. Feel your entire body relaxing.

Focus your attention on your hips and buttocks. Feel your buttocks resting on the chair. Relax your hips and buttocks.

Feel energy in you thigh, knee and legs. Stretch them extending outward then place back down. Feel your thighs, knees and legs relax.

Bring your attention to your ankles and feet, feel the bottom of your feet on the floor, relax your ankles, relax your feet.

Gently return your attention to the tip of your nose, to your nostrils.

Feel breath entering your nostrils, feel breath leaving your nostrils, feel breath coming in and going out.

Focus your attention on this breathing for 3-4 breaths, then breathe normally.

Now, imagine you see a movie screen unrolling before you.

A thick white mist appears swirling all around the screen.

Bliss Balling No.1 - Health

AS THE MIST CLEARS
See yourself seated at a table.
Imagine you see hundreds of tiny specks of light dissolving
as they fall on and around you.
Lights are everywhere!
These tiny lights are Bliss balls of joy.
Cup your hands, watch as Bliss balls land in your palms
dissolving into each other.

Use your imagination to:
Merge your body with the image of you holding and gazing
at the Bliss balls dissolving in your hands.
As you merge, a tiny gold seed with writing on it falls
from the Bliss ball onto the table.
Pick up the seed marked Health, drop it on the Bliss ball.
Watch it dissolve into the light.
Bliss ball glows brighter, feel your body revitalize itself.
Feel energy pulsating through your body,
you feel healthy, happy and calm.

Place your bright, glowing Bliss ball down so it can grow.

Watch your Bliss ball growing,
getting bigger, taller, wider and brighter.
It becomes a ball of white light.

Imagine yourself stepping into the center of the white light.
Take a moment, imagine what perfect health means to you.

Now inhale and exhale white light
slowly through your nostrils.
Feel Bliss ball being absorbed by your body.
Watch as light of your Bliss ball dissolves
completely into your body.
Know that you carry joy and perfect health within you.
Know that your Bliss ball can be called upon,
for health anytime
using the power of your imagination.

Open your eyes, go about your day.

Bliss Balling No. 2 – Love

AS THE MIST CLEARS
See yourself seated at a table.
Imagine you see hundreds of tiny specks of light dissolving
as they fall on and around you.
Lights are everywhere!
These tiny lights are Bliss balls of joy.
Cup your hands, watch as Bliss balls land in your palms
dissolving into each other.

Use your imagination to:
Merge your body with the image of you holding
and gazing at the Bliss balls dissolving in your hands.
As you merge, a tiny gold seed with writing on it falls
from the Bliss ball onto the table.

Pick up the seed marked Love, watch it dissolve in the light,
See the Bliss ball become larger and brighter.
Place your bright, glowing Bliss ball down.
Watch your Bliss ball growing, getting bigger,
taller, wider and brighter.
It becomes a ball of white light.

Imagine yourself stepping into the center of the white light.
Think: what love means to and for you.
Hold those thoughts and feelings for a few moments.
Now inhale and exhale white light
slowly through your nostrils.
Feel Bliss ball being absorbed by your body.
Watch as light of your Bliss ball
dissolves completely into your body.
Know that you carry joy and perfect love within you.
Know that you can call upon your Bliss ball of love anytime
using the power of your imagination.

Open your eyes, go about your day.

Bliss Balling No. 3 – Money

AS THE MIST CLEARS
See yourself seated at a table.
Imagine you see hundreds of tiny specks of light dissolving
as they fall on and around you.
Lights are everywhere!
These tiny lights are Bliss balls of joy.
Cup your hands, watch as Bliss balls land in your palms
dissolving into each other.
Use your imagination to:
Merge your body with the image of you holding
and gazing at the Bliss balls dissolving in your hands.
As you merge, a tiny gold seed with writing on it falls
from the Bliss ball onto the table.

Place Money seed on Bliss ball.
See it sizzle as it dissolves in the light.
Watch your Bliss ball growing, getting bigger,
taller, wider and brighter.
It becomes a ball of white light.
Imagine yourself stepping into the center of the white light.
Think about all the ways money can come to you.
Imagine you have become a money magnet.
Feel the pressure of money in your pockets.
See, feel the thickness of the bills in your hands.
Imagine the feeling of financial freedom.

Now inhale and exhale white light
slowly through your nostrils.
Feel Bliss ball being absorbed by your body.
Watch as light of your Bliss ball dissolves
completely into your body.
Know that you carry joy and money within you.
Know that you can call upon your Bliss ball
for money anytime
using the power of your imagination.

Open your eyes, go about your day.

Bliss Balling No. 4 – Success

AS THE MIST CLEARS
See yourself seated at a table.
Imagine you see hundreds of tiny specks of light dissolving
as they fall on and around you.
Lights are everywhere!
These tiny lights are Bliss balls of joy.
Cup your hands, watch as Bliss balls land in your palms
dissolving into each other.

Use your imagination to:
Merge your body with the image of you holding
and gazing at the Bliss balls dissolving in your hands.
As you merge, a tiny gold seed with writing on it falls
from the Bliss ball onto the table.

Place the Success seed on the pulsating Bliss ball.
Hear sirens as Success dissolves into the light.
Place your bright, glowing Bliss ball down.
Watch your Bliss ball growing, getting bigger,
taller, wider and brighter.
It becomes a ball of white light.

Imagine yourself stepping into the
center of the ball of white light.
Sense a feeling of confidence, security and prosperity.
Imagine the successful completion
of your desires one by one.
See your successes.
Now inhale and exhale white light
slowly through your nostrils.
Feel Bliss ball being absorbed by your body.
Watch as light of your Bliss ball dissolves
completely into your body.
Know that you carry success within you.
Know that you can call upon your
Bliss ball for success anytime

using the power of your imagination.

Open your eyes, go about your day.

TAKE 2 MINUTES

If you don't have 15 minutes to spare for meditation, take two minutes a few times a day. You must first get your body and mind in the habit of relaxing. The habit can be achieved by practicing the relaxation portion of Bliss Balling. Relaxation feels different from being tired or sleepy. Relaxation is a process of mind where you are consciously communicating an action to each part of your body. Two minutes can be taken a few times a day to refresh the body and mind, for peace in your space or success in some activity. In two minutes, you are exercising your powers of imagination, meditation, belief, thought, word and repetition at the same time.

Take 2-minutes: Directions: The relaxation process is always the same. You'll start by getting comfortable where you will not be disturbed; seated with feet flat on floor, hands open on lap and eyes closed. With deep breath no. 1: imagine your head, scalp, eyelids, jaw, throat and neck, relaxing. Deep breath no. 2: feel your shoulders, arms, chest, hands, relax. Deep breath no. 3: imagine your solar plexus, hips, spine, buttocks, thighs, relax. Deep breath no. 4: feel your legs, knees, ankles, feet, relax. Deep breath no. 5: allow entire body to relax. Deep breath no. 6: feel your entire body relaxing. Begin normal breathing for the next 12 breaths.

To refresh or energize your body: Begin normal breathing while visualizing yourself standing in white light or the light of the sun receiving that energy. Hold the thought or keep repeating that one thought for 12 normal breaths. Initially, you may have to use your fingers to count out 12 breaths until you have trained your body and mind to know when the minute is up. Then, open your eyes and go about your day.

For anything you desire, simply imagine your desire fulfilled. For any success, the end or result of that success must be visualized. In other words, see yourself enjoying or experiencing your completed desire. Use one word or one thought, keeping this as simple as possible and do it as often as you can. With practice, you'll know exactly when 12 breaths or the minute is up.

There is only one way to know the value of the material in this book and that is to test it for yourself.

Made in the USA
Monee, IL
07 July 2026

56551290R00050